Options Trading Course

The Essential Guide For Investing With Options, Generating A Consistent Cash Flow Without Effort, And Generate Passive Income With Low Risks

Byron McGrady

Table of Contents

Introduction

Options Trading is a great way to get involved in the world of finance without the heavy learning curve. If you want to get involved in the world of Options Trading, but don't know where to begin.

It is one of the most profitable and exciting ways to earn money. Although options trading can be complicated, it is not difficult to understand. In this article, we'll cover the basics, strategies, and information you need to know about options trading.

Options trading is similar to investing in stocks and bonds, except instead of buying shares of a company or buying paper for cash; you are buying an option on it.

Options are financial securities that give the holder the right to buy or sell a particular asset at a specific price and date.

Options have been traded since the dawn of civilization. Invented in 1801 by a French financier named Pierre de Fermat, options were initially used as a form of investment instrument to speculate on future stock market movements.

It can be used to gain exposure to particular asset classes without having to purchase the underlying investments. They also provide traders with an opportunity to control their risk when trading a high-risk investment asset. It is important to note that options were traded before they were invented.

The first documented use of options occurred over 2,000 years ago during Roman times.

Options trading made its way into the United States in 1790 when pioneers brought it from England with them when they migrated across the Atlantic Ocean. The term option was coined in 1790 by Alexander Hamilton, who wrote that "a merchant can be made to owe his entire fortune to an option."

Options trading is an innovative way to invest in the market. Traders can profit from both rising and falling prices of stocks.

Trading options can be extremely profitable for experienced traders who know how to manage risk and choose to open and close their positions. Options trading also offers investors an opportunity to own shares in what otherwise may be extremely volatile stock markets such as Brazil's Ibo Vespa or China's Shanghai Composite Index. Those who trade options regularly can be financially rewarding to see the value of their investment double overnight when a company goes public or is bought out by another company.

Options trading continues to gain popularity. It is becoming easier for first-time investors to enter this lucrative market through online brokerages, and discount brokerages like Options Trading Crash Course Online Brokerage (Options Trading Crash Course).

CHAPTER 1:

Trading Psychology

We associate trading psychology to some behaviors and emotions that are often the triggers for catalysts for decisions. The most common emotions that every trader will come across are fear and greed.

Fear

At any given time, fear represents one of the worst kinds of emotions that you can have. Check-in your newspaper one day, and you read about a steep selloff, and the next thing is trying to rack your brain about what to do next, even if it isn't the right action at that time.

Many investors think that they know what will happen in the following few days, which makes them have a lot of confidence in the trade outcome. It leads to investors getting into the trade at a level that is too high or too low, which in turn makes them react emotionally.

As the trader puts a lot of hope on the single trade, the level of fear tends to increase, and hesitation and caution kick in.

Fear is part of every trader, but skilled traders can manage the fear. There are various types of fears that you will experience:

The Fear to Lose

Have you ever entered a trade and all you could think about is losing? The fear of losing makes it hard for you to execute the perfect strategy or enter or exit a strategy at the right time.

As a trader, you know that you need to make timely decisions when the strategy signals you to take one. When fear guiding you, the level of confidence drops, and you can't execute the strategy the right way, at the right time. When a strategy fails, you lose trust in your abilities as well as strategy.

When you lose trust in many of the strategies, you end up with analysis paralysis, whereby you can't pull the trigger on any decision you make. Making a move becomes a huge challenge.

When you cannot pull the trigger, all you can think about is staying away from the pain of loss while you need to move towards gains.

No trader likes to lose, but it is a fact that even the best traders will make losses once in a while. The key is for them to make more profitable trades that allow them to stay in the game.

When you worry too much, you end up being distracted from your execution process, and instead, you focus on the results.

To reduce the fear of trading, you need to accept losses. The probability of losing or making a profit is 50/50, and you need to get this fact and accept a trade, whether it is a sell or a buy signal.

The Fear of a Positive Trend Going Negative (and Vice Versa)

Many traders choose to go for quick profits, and then leave the losses to run down. Many traders want to convince themselves that they have made some money for the day, so they tend to go for a quick profit to have the winning feeling.

So, what should you do instead? You need to stick with the trend. When you notice a trend is starting, it is good to stay with the trend until you signal that the trend is about to reverse. It is only then that you exit this position.

To understand this concept, you need to consider the history of the market. History is good at pointing out that times change, and trends can go either way. Remember that no one knows the exact time the trend will start or end; all you need to do is wait upon the signal.

The Fear of Missing Out

For every trade, you have people that doubt the capacity of the trade to go through. After you place the trade, you will be faced with many skeptics that will question the whole procedure and leave you wondering whether to exit the strategy or not.

This fear is also characterized by greed because you aren't working on the premise of making a successful trade rather the fact that the security is rising without you having a piece of the pie.

This fear is usually based on information that you missed a trend that you would have capitalized on.

This fear has a downside, you will forget about any potential risk associated with the trade, and instead, think that you can make a profit because other people benefited from the action.

Fear of Being Wrong

Many traders put too much emphasis on being right that they forget that this is a business they should run the right way. They also forget that being successful is all about knowing the trend and how it affects their engagement.

When you follow the best timing strategy, you create many positive results over a specific time.

The uncanny desire to focus on always being right instead of focusing on making money is a great part of your ego, and to stay on the right path, you need to trade without your ego for once.

If you accommodate a perfectionist mentality when you get into trades, you will be after failure because you will experience many losses. Perfectionists don't take losses the right way, and this translates into fear.

Ways to Overcome Fear in Trading

As you can see, it is evident that fear can lead to losses. So, how can you avoid this fear and become successful?

Learn

You need to find a way to get knowledge so that you have the basis for making decisions. When you know all there is to know about options, you know what to buy and when to sell, and learn which ones to watch. You are then more comfortable making the right decisions.

Have Goals

What are your short-term and long-term goals? Setting the right goals helps you to overcome fear. When you have goals, you have rules that dictate how you behave, even in times of fear. You also have a timeline for your journey.

Envision the Bigger Picture

You always need to evaluate your choices at all times and see what you have gained or lost so far for taking some steps. Understanding the mistakes, you made guides you to make better decisions in the future.

Start Small

Many traders that subscribe to fear have lost a lot before. They put many funds on the line and ended up losing, which made them fear to place other trades. Begin with small sums so that you don't risk too much to put fear in you. Once you get more confident, you can invest more considerable sums so that you enjoy more profit.

Use the Right Strategy

Having the right trading strategy makes it easy to execute your trades successfully. Make sure you look at various options trading strategies to know which one is ideal for your situation and skills.

Many strategies can help you succeed, but others might leave you confused. If you have a strategy that doesn't give you the returns you desire, then adjust it to suit your needs over time. Refine it till you are comfortable with its performance.

Go Simple

When you have a simple and straightforward strategy, you will be less likely to lose confidence along the way because you know what to expect. The easier the strategy, the faster it will be to spot any issues.

Don't Hesitate

At times you have to jump into the fray even if you aren't so comfortable with the way it works. Once you begin taking steps, you will learn more about the trade.

You always need to be prepared when taking any trade. The more prepared you are, the easier it will be for you to run successful trades.

Don't Give Up

Some things might not go as you expect them to do. Remember that mistakes are there to give you lessons that will make you a better trader. When you lose, take time to identify the mistake you made and then correct it, then try again.

Greed

This refers to a selfish desire to get more money than you need from a trade. When the desire to get more than you can usually make takes over your decision-making process, you are looking at failure.

Greed is seen to be more detrimental than fear. Yes, fear can make you lose trades, but the good thing is that you get to preserve your capital. On the other hand, greed places you in a situation where you spend your capital faster than you return. It pushes you to act when you shouldn't be acting at all.

The Danger of Being Greedy

When you are greedy, you end up acting irrationally. Irrational trading behavior can be overtrading, overleveraging, holding onto trades for too long, or chasing different markets.

The more greed you have, the more foolish you act. If you reach a point at which greed takes over from common sense, you are overdoing it.

When you are greedy, you also risk much more than you can handle, and you end up with a loss. You also have unrealistic expectations from the market, making it seem as if you are after just money and nothing else.

When you are greedy, you also start trading prematurely without any knowledge of the options trading market.

When you are too greedy, your judgment is clouded, and you won't think about any negative consequences that might result when you make certain decisions.

Many traders that were too greedy ended up giving up after making this mistake in the initial trading phase.

How to Overcome Greed

You need a lot of effort to overcome greed. It might not be easy because we are talking about human emotions here, but it is possible.

First, you have to know that every call you make won't be the right one at all times. There are times when you won't make the right move, and you will end up losing money. At times you will miss the perfect strategy altogether and you won't move a step ahead.

Secondly, you have to agree that the market is way bigger than you. When you do this, you will accept and make mistakes in the process.

Hope

Hope is what keeps a trading expectation alive when it has reached reversal. It is usually factored in a trader's mind that has placed a huge amount on a trade. Many traders also go for hope when they wish to recoup past losses. These traders are always hopeful that the next trade will be the best, and they end up placing more than they should on the trade.

This emotion is dangerous because the market doesn't care about your hopes and will take your money.

Regret

This is the feeling of disappointment or sadness over a trade that has been done, especially when it has resulted in a loss.

Focusing too much on missing trade makes the trader not to move forward. After you learn the lessons after such a loss, you need to understand the mistakes you made then move ahead.

When you decide to let regret rule your thinking, you start chasing markets, hoping that you will make money on a position by doubling the entrance price.

CHAPTER 2:

Risk Management in Options Trading

Trading is generally not without risk, and options pose a higher risk than other forms of securities. The risk is mostly due to its speculative nature. As a trader, you need to protect yourself and trading capital from unnecessary losses, and any potential losses that can be prevented.

We do not engage in trades to lose money. A lot of beginners lose money in their early days. Some believe that this is an inevitable process. However, it does not have to be this way. With proper planning and especially proper risk management, you should not unnecessarily lose money trading the markets.

Your number one focus should be risk management rather than winning trades or strategies to be successful as a trader. A good trader is one who does not unnecessarily lose money. The most successful traders manage their funds so well they always know how much to spend or hold back. To do this, you have to watch your every move and countercheck every decision that you make. For instance, if you want to enter a market position, you need to ask yourself if that move is necessary and what amounts you stand to lose should it not work out.

Effective Risk Management

The options trading process does carry some risks with it. Understanding these risks and taking mitigating steps will make you not just a better trader but a more profitable one as well. Many traders love options trade because of the immense leverage that this kind of trading affords them. Should an investment work out as desired, then the profits are often relatively high. You can expect returns of between 10%, 15%, or even 20% with stocks. However, when it comes to options, profit margins of more than 1,000% are possible.

We are familiar with bad investments and losses emanating from individuals or organizations that were hoping to be profitable. Numerous traders make huge errors when they trade, resulting in significant losses. This only happens when they know not what they are doing and when they do not take sufficient steps to protect themselves.

Remember that profits do not just show up. It takes plenty of hard work and, most of all, proper risk management techniques. Without risk management techniques, there is no need to enter the markets because you will be risking your funds. Keep in mind that trading options are a highly risky venture because it is speculative. As such, you cannot trade without protecting yourself. Here are ways you can protect yourself and your trading capital.

Have a Trading Plan

This cannot be mentioned enough times. One of the most important things is to have a trading plan. This plan details exactly all the steps that you will follow from market entry to exit. You should sit down and consider all possible scenarios.

There is no need to take any risks. Once you learn as much as you can about options and trading, you should learn how to plan your trades. Wise traders say anyone who fails to plan is planning to fail. If you want to succeed, you should develop a trading plan that you should then abide by. Again, there is no need to develop a trading plan if you will not implement it fully.

A trading plan's primary purpose is to ensure that you manage your money wisely and place it only well-planned and well-executed strategies. This way, you will avoid reckless moves and only put your money in strategies well worked out.

All too often, a trader will enter a trade without understanding exactly how it will play out. In such instances, the chances of losing money are incredibly high. If you are unsure about any move, then please do not make it. A single move could imply a risk. With a good plan, all moves will be calculated, and no unnecessary risks will be taken.

Understand Trading Psychology

Trading options largely revolves around three significant factors. These are money management, trading strategies, and psychology. Keep in mind that the markets can be a very emotional place, so you must remain focused and disciplined. If you do not stay disciplined, you will lose out, and others will likely take advantage of you.

You need to trade successfully to have a solid strategy, follow the strategy, and stick to it. If the strategy does not follow the intended plan, then quit and develop another strategy.

If you have a strong mindset, you will understand when to pursue a losing trade and when to quit. If you lack discipline, then one of two emotions will take over. These are greed and fear.

Sometimes traders trade on a whim and keep posting random trades. Rather than take this approach, you really should focus on a successful strategy which you will pursue until you need to exit. You should also have good trading skills and a proper money management plan. With these in place, you will focus better and think in terms of probabilities, and risk-reward ratios. This way, you will not leave room for emotional trading.

There are other things that you need to also keep in mind. For instance, you need to develop and stick with good trading habits.

As a trader, you need to note that a winner is one who is persistent and consistent. You should develop the habit of closely studying the markets, conducting your analysis, and position sizing.

Position sizing is crucial, especially in a volatile market. As such, you need to take care of your downside risks and ensure that your position size appropriate. You should also envision the end game. See a vision of where you want the trade to head, and then prepare to make any necessary adjustments.

You also need to accept any possible failures. Sometimes your strategies will not work out, and you will lose some trades. This happens to all traders, even experienced ones. If you assume that you must succeed on each attempt, you will set yourself up for failure.

Risks are Inherent

All types of investing opportunities carry a certain level of risk. However, trading options carry a much higher risk of loss. Therefore, ensure that you have a thorough understanding of the risks, and always be on the lookout.

Also, these kinds of trades are possible due to the nature and leverage offered by options. A savvy trader realizes that they can control an almost equivalent number of shares as a traditional stock investor but at a fraction of the cost. Therefore, when you invest in options, you can spend a tiny amount of money to control a large number of shares. This kind of leverage limits your risks and exposure compared to a stock investor.

Time is not on your side

All options have an expiration date. When you invest in stocks, time is on your side most of the time. However, things are different when it comes to options. The closer an option gets to its expiration, the quicker it loses its value and earning potential.

Options deterioration is usually rather rapid, and it accelerates in the last days until expiration. As an investor, ensure that you only invest dollar amounts that you can afford to lose. The good news, though, is that there are a couple of actions that you can take to get things on your side.

Therefore, try and always or at least mostly to choose options whose expiry dates lie within your investment opportunity. Also, identify options that are at the money or very close. These increase your chances of profitability while minimizing risks and exposure. Ensure that you sell options whenever you believe that high prices are due to volatility. Instead, choose to purchase options when you believe that volatility is undervalued.

Naked Short Positions Can Result in Substantial Losses

Anytime you decide to short options naked, this presents a high likelihood of substantial and sometimes even unlimited losses. Shorting put naked means selling stock options with no hedging of your position.

When selling a naked short, it simply implies that you are actually selling a call option or even a put option but without securing it using an option position, stock, or cash. It is advisable to sell a put or a call-in combination with other options or with stocks. Remember that whenever you short sell a stock, you are, in essence, selling borrowed stock. Sooner or later, you will have to return the stock.

Fortunately, with options, there is no borrowing of stock or any other security.

Prices can Move Pretty Fast

Options are highly leveraged financial instruments. Because of this, prices tend to move pretty fast. Options prices can move huge amounts within minutes and sometimes even seconds. This is unlike other stock market instruments like stocks that move-in hours and days.

When structuring your options, you should ensure that you use the correct strike prices, and expiration months to cut out most of the risk. You should also consider closing out your trades well before the expiration of options. This way, the time value will not dramatically deteriorate.

CHAPTER 3:

Trading Option to Gain Financial Freedom

The path of options trading is simple but not easy. However, you can make it work in significant ways. All you need is the discipline, determination, skills, and ambition that will enable you to navigate this journey.

You must develop the qualities that all successful options traders have. Qualities such as patience, perseverance, flexibility, meticulousness, optimism, discipline, and you must be capable of managing risk. You need to know your numbers and never allow yourself to become complacent. Complacency is the enemy of financial success in this game. You also need to have clear specific financial goals and keep your eye focused on the end goal.

The seven stages of financial freedom:

Stage one: Gain clarity

You need to know where you are and identify where you want to be. What are your expenses like? Can you cut back on certain things so you can have more to invest in? What's the current state of your credit card statement? Financial experts recommend having a particular budget for your life.

Having a budget for your life and options trading activities, so you monitor each closely. Track all your expenses, and once you're clear on what you owe, where you will cut back, and where you want to be soon, you're ready for the second stage.

Remember, you need to be specific with the exact amount of money you want to have in your account at the end of this year, five and ten years from now.

Stage two: Self-sufficiency

The next step is to learn to provide for yourself. There's no attaining financial freedom if you don't know how to earn enough so that you can live on your terms and cater to your needs. This level requires many sacrifices, but if you have that big picture driving you, it won't be too hard to make it work.

Stage three: Breathing room

This is the stage where you earn enough to provide and start saving some money. After you have saved up for months' worth of expenses, you can finally begin to have enough room to breathe.

Stage four: Stability

This is where you increase your savings to a year and knowing that you'll be good for a year helps you feel grounded and secure.

Stage five: Flexibility

It is the last level of saving that you'll need to do. Go ahead and save up two years' worth of expenses so you can feel completely protected and free enough to live how you want. You now have the flexibility you've always dreamed of, and you can start reassessing your priorities.

Stage six: Financial independence

Life is delightful at this stage because you know you have enough money to last you for the rest of your life. Sabatier recommends investing in income-producing assets to achieve financial independence or saving a million dollars then living off your investment interest. Of course, as options traders, we know investing in options can get us to financial independence faster than any of his methods.

Stage seven: Abundant wealth

At this stage of your financial journey, you are not only free, but you also have the means and power to be, do, have, and give whatever you want to share with the world. It's where you can start thinking about your legacy, and the difference you want to make in the world. If you have a favorite cause that you wish to support or create a foundation of your own or whatever your dream is, this is where it all turns into reality. If you're on a mission to do something meaningful in this world, having an abundance of wealth is an advantage that will guarantee you achieve that mission. The moment money stops being a source of stress in your life, you will unlock more potential, resources, and creativity from within you that you never thought possible.

If you play the game right in the long run, and you stick to your vision, mission, and plan options, trading can help you manifest your dream life sooner rather than later.

At the end of the day, although there are many different paths to get to the top and no one-size-fits-all strategy or plan can work across the board for all traders, they all have one thing in common is the right mindset. All successful traders work hard to keep upgrading and maintain the right mindset.

We must continuously work on our mindset to withstand and rise above the daily challenges of options trading. Certain qualities are inherent and nurtured by all successful traders. Still, you also need to remember that putting in the work and keep a level head are equally as important as having those qualities such as discipline, persistence, perseverance, etc.

Work on upgrading your mindset. Feed your mind good food just as you feed your body good food. Work on your weaknesses; get to know the habits that hinder you and those that foster success. Double down on your strengths and developmental resilience. You need to manage your mental activity and energy better if you want to master this trading game. So be mindful and watchful of your behavior as you study and start trading.

Once you identify your thought patterns and start course correction, everything else you do will begin to pay off in a big way.

CHAPTER 4:

LEAPS

LEAPS (Long-term Equity Anticipation Security) are long-term options with expiration dates of up to 3 years, commonly expiring in January.

Ex-Dividend Date/Ex-Date

This term is the day before the date on which the investor had to buy the stock to gather the dividend. On the ex-dividend date, the earlier day's price is decreased by the amount of the premium because the purchaser collects the dividend payment on the ex-dividend date, and it will not receive it. This date is usually referred to as an ex-date and should apply to many other situations (e.g., splits, distributions). If you purchase a stock on the ex-date for a stock or a distribution, you will not be entitled to the split stock or distribution. Nevertheless, the stock's opening price would be decreased by a large amount, as at the ex-dividend date.

Exchange-Traded Funds (ETFs)

These are index funds or trusts enlisted on an exchange and traded in a manner almost like that of single equity. The first ETF came into being in 1993 with the AMEX's concept of a tradable stock basket: Standard and Poor's Depositary Receipt (SPDR).

The numbers of ETFs that trade options grow continuously and diversify today. Investors can buy or sell shares within the whole stock portfolio (or bond portfolio) as one security. Exchange-traded funds help investors enjoy a number of the more desirable stock trading features, just like the simple equity style and liquidity, in a more conventional index investing setting.

Fence

Options could have the same or different strike prices. The months of expiration may or might not be the same. For example, if the investor had formerly purchased ABC Corporation at $46 and increased to $62, the investor would be ready to create a collar involving the buying of a put for May 60, and the writing of a call for May 65 as a way of preserving a number of the unrealized profits in the stock position of ABC Corporation. An investor can also use the reverse, i.e., a long call combined with a written put if he has initially established a brief stock position in ABC Corporation.

Holder

A holder is one that has made a gap purchase transaction, put or call, and holds that position in a brokerage account.

Mark-To-Market

This manner implies an accounting mechanism whereby the price of securities held in an account is valued daily to represent the price or market quotes. As a result, the equity within the account is updated daily to represent current security prices appropriately.

Market Order

This word is a trading order issued to a broker to immediately purchase or sell a stock or an option at the best price available.

OTC Option

The over-the-counter option is traded on the OTC market. These options are not listed on an exchange of options and do not have standard terms. These are to be differentiated from the exchange-listed and traded standard equity options.

In-The-Money Option

The term is used to define an option with an intrinsic value. When the stock price is above the strike price, a call option is said to be in-the-money. The put option is in-the-money if the stock price is a smaller amount than the strike price.

Out-Of-The-Money Option

This word is a term used to describe an option that does not have an intrinsic value. The premium for the option is value. In ordinary contracts, the call option is out-of-the-money if the stock price is below its strike price. The put option is out-of-the-money when the stock price is above its strike price.

Naked or Uncovered Option

This word is a short option position that is not entirely protected if assignment notification is received. A short call position is claimed to be uncovered when the author does not have a long stock or deeper in-the-money long call position. A short put is uncovered when the author does not have a brief stock or an extended deeper in-the-money position.

The Role of Underlying Stocks

The underlying asset is a financial asset on which the price of the derivative is predicated. Options are examples of a derivative. A derivative is a financial tool that has a price that is based on a particular asset.

Underlying assets give value to derivatives. For example, the stock ABC option gives the holder right to buy or sell ABC at the strike price up till the expiration date. The stock of XYZ is that the underlying asset for the option.

The underlying asset could also be used to identify an item within the agreement that adds value to the contract. This way supports the security involved in the contract, in which the parties involved make a covenant to exchange as a part of the derivative contract.

Derivative Contracts

This product is an option price or derivative instrument springs of the underlying asset. In an option contract, the author has got to either purchase or sell the underlying asset to the purchaser on the required date at an agreed price. The buyer is not obliged to buy the asset, but they can use their right if they need to do so. Suppose the option is about expiring, and the underlying asset has not progressed favorably enough to render exercising of the option worthwhile. In that case, the purchaser may allow it to expire and lose the amount paid for the option.

A future is an obligation to the buyer and the seller. The longer-term vendor decides to provide the underlying asset at the expiration, and the buyer agrees to get the underlying asset at the expiry. The price they earn and pay is when they have entered into a futures contract. Many futures traders chose to close their positions before the expiration date. But they will buy or sell a contract at a specific price, and if it changes favorably, they will get out of the trade and earn a profit that way. A future is a derivative since, for instance, the price of an oil derivative instrument depends on the movement of oil prices.

Example of Underlying Assets

The underlying asset is the stock, in the case of stock options. For example, with an option to purchase 100 shares of Company A at $100, the underlying asset is that the stock of Company A. That determines the option's price up to its expiration date. This value could change, influencing the cost of the option before the contract expires. At any given time, the underlying asset's price helps traders know whether or not the choice is worth exercising.

A stock market index (or currency like S&P 500) can also be an asset. In the stock indexes, the asset consists of common stocks in the stock exchange index.

CHAPTER 5:

Methods of Buying Options

Buyers of call options view the marketplace cost of a specific stock and are looking to benefit from this predicted increase in market price.

The most well-known technique for buying call options is speculating on a boost in the underlying stock market. It is an essential strategy that is more popular than purchasing put options, as it is more easily comprehended.

Purchasing Options

When buying call options, you hypothesize that the underlying stock rate will increase substantially within the restricted time duration to produce revenue. The percentage returns on your trade if you are proven proper are enormous. If you are incorrect, you can lose some or all of the premium initial you paid.

Buying the right to you is to purchase 100 shares of the underlying stock at the strike cost before the expiry date. You pay a premium for this right. Once you have bought your option, you have three options:

- Sell your options before expiry.

- Exercise your options before expiration.

- Allow the option to expire worthlessly.

The action you take will rely on the movement in the market rate of the hidden share, your expectation of any future motion before expiry, your factors for purchasing the call, and your danger tolerance.

Time is a substantial aspect of figuring out how you manage your options trade. Everyday options that you hold, the value time of your option will decrease. And it will reduce at an increasing rate as you approach the expiration date. In truth, even if the market price of the underlying stock increases before expiry, you might still lose cash on your option due to the impact of time decay, counteracting any increase in intrinsic value.

Methods for purchasing call options

How can you have the money lost on your option when the underlying stock's market cost has risen?

When you bought your option, it was at-the-money. As a result, the overall option premium of $3.50 consisted of time worth. Even though the stock cost increased by $2.00, and your option's intrinsic worth increased by $2.00, this was offset by a time decay of $3.50.

- Increase in intrinsic value$ 2.00.

- Decline in time value ($ 3.50).

- Your net loss on the options *($ 1.50).

This estimation does not consist of deal costs. The above example shows that to earn a profit on buying a call OPTION, the marketplace worth of the underlying stock requirements to increase by enough to both:

- Balanced out the time decay.

- Create development in the intrinsic value of the option.

There are several factors why you may think about buying call options as your trading technique. These include the following:

Method 1: Gain Use

Purchasing call options give you an advantage in your profit. You only need to provide small capital to purchase call options compared to buying the stock entirely. It also allows you to increase the portion of your returns.

Method 2: Limit Your Danger

Instead of acquiring the stock directly, getting call options also allows you to limit your losses if the stock cost falls. You might wish to speculate on a boost in the market worth of a specific stock; however, you might also not want to be exposed to prospective losses if the marketplace value falls considerably. If the stock you purchase, you are exposed to the full quantity of any fall in the stock cost. Nevertheless, with call options, you can ever lose the premium you paid, despite how far the stock rate might fall.

Method 3: Postpone A Stock Purchase

Once you buy a call option, you are purchasing the right to buy 100 shares of the primary stock at the strike price before the expiry date or anytime. Therefore, you are securing the rate you will pay for the shares if you decide to work out the option and buy it before the options' expiry date.

You may want to invest long term in a specific stock as you feel it will increase in worth; nevertheless, you wish to delay your purchase for some factor. Or perhaps you want to buy the stock; however, it wishes to increase in worth to confirm your analysis of an anticipated price boost. Buying a call option permits you to postpone your purchase but still lock in the price you will acquire the stock. The marketplace has experienced some substantial falls in value recently, and you wish to take advantage of the price depression. There is a stock single you have been watching before the fall, was trading over $30 per share, and is now trading at merely $18 per share. You think that the cost will rebound; however, you do not have the funds offered.

You choose to buy a $19 call option that has five months to expiry. The premium is $1. This purchase lets you acquire the stock at $19 per share whenever in the following five months. You have five months to raise funds to purchase the shares, and still purchase them at $19. Based upon what the stock rate does over this time, you can choose to offer your call options or exercise your call options, and buy the stock at $19.

Method 4: Hypothesize for Profit

A significant factor for buying call options is hypothesizing to generate short-term revenue. You are just speculating on the cost of the underlying stock rising by enough totals up to make earnings on your options. You are not acquiring the call options with any intent to exercise them.

Time decay will trigger the call options worth to fall as long as you are holding the option. For this factor, you need to be mindful of selecting the call options you wish to trade. You will require to stabilize the time you need for the stock to move in your instructions against the time value (expense) in the options premium.

You likewise require considering the strike price concerning the current market price of the stock underlying. You need options to be in-the-money to produce a boost in intrinsic worth. Call options will be more affordable when they are out-of-the-money, as more extensive price motion is needed to generate the option's inherent value. Conditions you should search for in selecting a call option for speculation consist of:

The strike price needs to be close to the current market value of the stock. When they are in-the-money options, this will ensure that the boost in the underlying stock cost will be shown in your option's price.

The expiry time must be extended enough for your stock cost to increase adequately to balance out the time decay and create a profit on your call options.

CHAPTER 6:

Financial Leverage in Options Trading

When you engage in options trading, you participate in what is called financial leverage. Financial leverage refers to the concept that instead of buying the stock outright and paying the full share price amount, you can put up an initial less capital. Based on the type of your options trade, you can enhance the return on your equity within or after the set time frame. Often, the amount of capital you leverage is lower than the actual share price of the stock. This apparent less capital is what gives options trading its appeal.

Advantages of Financial Leverage in Options Trading

1. You have rights. There are two types of options, both of which have rights: call option and put option. Call options allow you to buy shares at a given strike cost before the duration's expiry. On the other hand, put options will enable you to sell a specific amount of your stock at an agreed price any time within the trade contract's stipulated period.

2. You will own a given number of shares as stipulated in the options contract. We call it the option contract multiplier (most options have a multiplier of x100), which means you get to own 100 stock per option.

Any return on your prospect is factored into this multiplier, giving you an accurate figure on your overall investment return. This multiplier is the number of shares that your option contract can be converted into if you exercised that option. You can use your right to sell your trade contract at any time within the stipulated time frame if it is before the expiry date.

3. Your profit margins are highly magnified when compared to directly buying stocks and selling them at a profit later. In an options trading scenario, you leverage your investment at a given strike price against a future rise in the share price of that same stock price. Now, if the stock price rises as per your speculation, the return on your investment will be much higher than direct stock trading. Your profit margin ratio is much higher, as shown by this example:

Let us assume a current stock price of $20. A broker predicts the stock price to rise to $30 in a month. The trader issues a call option to buy the 20call for a $5 strike price, which expires in 1 month.

Given an option contract multiplier of 100, you can see below the marked difference in profit margin between direct stock trade of 100 shares, and options trade at the specified strike price.

If the final stock price is $30 in a month:

- Direct stock trade gives you a profit of $1000, 50% of the original investment.

- Options trade gives you a profit of $500, which is 100% of the initial investment.

If the final stock price is $35 in a month:

- Direct stock trade gives you a profit of $1500, which is 75% of the original investment.

- Options trade gives you a profit of $1000, which is 200% of the original investment.

4. Your initial cost is low. Buying options are less expensive than buying stock since it depends on the strike price at which you purchased the option. Buying stock depends on the stock price, which is usually markedly higher than the strike price. Therefore, it becomes favorable for you to buy a stake in the stock at a discounted rate.

5. Your call option value goes up whenever the share price rises above the stipulated initial cost.

6. Your put option value goes up as the share price falls below the stipulated initial cost.

7. You have an extra revenue stream. Profits from options trading are a source of income for your business.

Given the potential for much higher returns than conventional profit revenues, it gives you the ability to engage in more ambitious business endeavors.

8. Financial leverage in options trading allows you to settle debts incurred during the business. Your business may have a margin account used to accrue debt and leverage the debt in an options contract in anticipation of receiving markedly higher returns. Once you have taken care of liabilities, options trading gives you room to invest in other business opportunities.

Disadvantages of Financial Leverage in Options Trading

1. You have obligations when you sell, depending on your options. You are obligated to sell a specified number of shares for the determined amount whenever any call buyers trigger their contract when you are selling a call option. As a put option seller, you must buy a given number of stocks for a listed amount whenever any put buyers use their commitment. Your obligations force you to buy and sell at strike prices with much higher loss margins than if you had traded at the final stock prices.

2. Your get magnified losses. As much as your returns may have a higher profit margin, the same margin also applies to stock prices, which move in the opposite direction to the ones initially speculated. These losses have a significantly higher margin compared to losses incurred in cases of direct stock trading. You end up with disproportionate losses, which can leave you in financial ruin.

3. You are exposed to higher risks. Losing on your leverage does not depend on an unfavorable final stock price. In case your final stock price remains the same as the initial strike price by the end of the options period, you lose the whole of your initial investment. Using the earlier example, you can see this situation:

Given an option contract multiplier of 100, you can see the difference between the direct stock trade returns from 100 shares, and the effect on options trade when the stock price remains the same.

If the final stock price is $20 in a month:

- Direct stock trade gives you neither profit nor loss since the original investment remains unchanged.

- Options trade makes you lose your original investment of $500 since the call option becomes worthless at an unchanged final stock price.

It costs more to return to your original capital baseline. In cases where you incur losses, it will paradoxically cost you more to regain your initial investment. Look at the following example:

- If you had $1000 capital and lost 25%, you remain at $7500. Now, to regain your original money, you need to make a profit of $2500 from your existing $7500 (which means a return of 33% on $7500). You will need a much higher yield of 33% to cover an initial loss of 25%.

- Your put option loses value if the final share price rises above your specified initial value. Also, the closer you get to the option's expiration, the less valuable it becomes.

4. The value of your call option depreciates when the final share price goes below the initial cost amount.

5. Fear of the unknown. You depend on a chance or probability situation to go your way, and market forces have a nature of unpredictability. When leveraging high-risk accounts such as margin accounts, your debt liability increases significantly. You become overleveraged and possibly may lead you into bankruptcy.

6. You are contract-bound. The contract specifies the conditions and duration relating to the option. Terms become void once the expiration period has lapsed. When the market trend on stock prices is not going your way, you do not have the option of opting out to avoid further loss. You need to wait it out, and incur the full loss at the end of the specified period.

7. You may become addicted. Any situation in life, which promises the chance of a higher return from little or no input, is prone to be abused. When it comes to money, people's greed knows no bounds. A loss leads to a tendency to try to recover what was lost. The cycle becomes self-propagating.

8. Options trading in valued stock is expensive. Stocks with lower strike prices will cost you more because they are valuable to traders. Whenever you engage in financial leveraging within options trading, you will prefer to buy options at a much lower stock price,

increasing value. However, options that involve these highly volatile stocks are valuable and tend to cost you more.

9. You have a deadline. Every option trade has a specified time frame within which the financial leverage is of value. Beyond the expiration date, your options can no longer trade. There is a limited window for your stock to gain profit.

CHAPTER 7:

What is Forex

On the whole, the FOREX market functions like any other financial market. You have a series of buyers and sellers looking to make a profit buying and selling currency. In these transactions, you hope to buy at a lower price while hoping to sell at a higher price. That's all there is to it in terms of the day-to-day transactions that you will be making.

Beyond that, the intricacies of the FOREX market are based upon the currencies you are dealing with. In short, you are pitting one country's currency against other countries. This is why you need to be aware of the economic, political, and social issues that influence a nation's currency value. As such, this understanding will help you figure out how you can spot a potential profit.

Thus, to make a profit, you need to know how a currency's value is determined.

The value of a currency is set by the market. However, it's important to note that there needs to be a second currency to express the first value. It's like establishing the price of a pair of shoes. You need to use the currency to express the value of the shoes. Otherwise, it's impossible to determine the price. Sure, you could express it in terms of sugar, automobiles, or bottles of water, but that would be impractical.

The value of a currency is set just like any other commodity, through the market. The market is what enables a currency to have a specific market value. In general, this market value is expressed in US Dollars, as the US Dollar is the world reserve currency. Nevertheless, it is possible to express currencies in terms of any other currency. However, this can be a complex calculation, and it almost always involves pegging one currency to the US Dollar unless there is a specific calculation done among currencies. This is generally done among neighboring countries, especially when there is a large trade among them.

Currency Pairs

FOREX is based on currency pairs. This means that you can only trade two currencies at any one time. While it is entirely possible to place as many trades as you like, individual trades can only be conducted in two currencies. What this means is that you start with one currency and trade in another.

Common currency pairs are the US Dollar and the Euro, the Dollar and the Japanese Yen, the Euro and the Chinese Yuan, or the Dollars and the Swiss Franc. The British Pound Sterling is a commonly traded currency, though it isn't quite as predominant as the US Dollar. Virtually all investors speculate for or against the Dollar at any point.

We will assume that investors are holding US Dollars and will start trading in US Dollars. You can build up a position in any currency you feel would make a good profit for you. So, there is no restriction in that sense.

The mechanism that's used to calculate trades is known as the "exchange rate." The exchange rate is the value of one currency expressed in another. This is what you commonly see when you travel to another country. You need to exchange currency to purchase the local currency that you can use to buy and sell. This is the pricing mechanism that FOREX uses to calculate the magnitude of a trade.

In general, the more valuable currency will translate into a greater amount of the less valuable currency. For instance, currency A is more valuable than currency B. The exchange rate would reflect this as 2 to 1, that is, 1 unit of currency A gets you 2 units of currency B. When there is a 1 to 1 ratio, you assume that both currencies are worth the same. While this rarely happens in today's economy, it should be noted some currencies are close to a 1 to 1 ratio. There is very little room to make a profit unless you either invest a large sum or make multiple transactions that add up over time.

Fundamental Mechanics of FOREX Trading

So, let's assume that you are holding 100 US Dollars (USD). Since this is your starting point, you need to analyze which currency you wish to trade. In this case, let's consider the Euro (EUR) as it is the most commonly traded pair.

Let's assume there is a 1 to 1.10 exchange rate, meaning that 1 EUR will get you 1.10 USD. Therefore, the EUR is more valuable than the USD. When you take 100 USD and purchase EUR, you will receive 90.9 EUR. Now, to make money, you would have to speculate that the USD falls in value. Suppose the exchange rate is now 1 to 1.15. Under this assumption, the 90.9 EUR you have is now worth 104.54 USD. In this example, you stand to profit from 4.54 USD when you convert the EUR back into USD.

This transaction is an example of an investor betting against the USD. This is important because had the USD and the EUR went to a 1 to 1 ratio, and the investor would have lost 10 USD.

Also, this example highlights how you are only flipping one currency for another and back. This can work when working in market conditions where there is a relative amount of volatility, that is, changes in the exchange rates. This is what can allow you to make short-term gains. When you have relatively stable currency pairs, you may have to hold out a bit longer to make money.

Alternatively, you could trade USD into EUR and then take those EUR, and make another trade pitting another currency against the EUR. You are guessing that this particular currency would drop in value against the EUR, thereby making the EUR much more valuable against it. As you can see, these transactions can be as complex as you would like them to be.

It should also be noted that these transactions which we have described are known as the "spot" market. This means that all positions are settled in cash, and are based on the 1 to 1 trade of currency. This is important as there are various amounts of derivatives based on currency. Derivatives are contracts in which special agreements are made involving the currency. One such example is a futures contract. A futures contract is a guarantee to buy or sell a currency at some point in the future. This is ideal for individuals and companies that may need a foreign currency point in the future but may not be certain of it. It helps them lock in a specific exchange rate, especially when there is a large degree of uncertainty in the global market.

How to Get Started with FOREX Trading

Virtually all trading is now conducted electronically. The days of brokers pounding the trading floor are not quite as predominant as they once were. This means that you can trade in FOREX from the comfort of your home or office. However, it isn't quite as simple as that. You need to gain access to the FOREX marketplace through a trading platform. A trading platform is a piece of software that is used to conduct trades. Duly licensed financial institutions develop this platform. As such, you are granted access to this platform by the financial institution to trade on their behalf. In essence, this makes you a stockbroker. The difference is that you are not paying a professional money manager a commission to handle your funds. You are doing that on your own.

To get started with a FOREX trading platform, you can do a quick online search to find the options available to you. That's why it's up to you to conduct your own research so that you can find the one that offers you the best overall choice.

That being said, gaining access to a trading platform generally consists of purchasing a subscription. Subscriptions vary in cost and services offered. Generally speaking, they offer access to the trading platform in addition to analytics services. These analytics are used to conduct technical analysis and fundamental analysis. These types of analysis help you base your decision on statistical models. Please bear in mind that guessing will only lead you to subpar, if not disappointing, results.

Also, please ensure that you get all of the information regarding the cost of membership, a fee per trade (or transaction), and any minimum account balance that you need to maintain. Please note that if transaction fees are high, these may end up zapping your profits.

Reasons Why FOREX Is a Good Investment Opportunity

Unlike other investment opportunities such as day and swing trading, FOREX offers a greater deal of flexibility, and the chance to make sizeable returns. Day trading generally consumes a lot of time in terms of research and actual trading. Day traders are subject to market hours and need to place trades at the beginning and the end of the day. Otherwise, they may leave positions open or risk losing on their deals due to overnight trading.

With FOREX, you don't need to invest a great deal of money. Most FOREX trading accounts have minimums of $300 to $500. While that's not chump change, it pales in comparison to the thousands of dollars that professional day traders move around on a single day. The best part of FOREX trading is that you can conduct trades for a few minutes at a time, cash out, and be certain that you know exactly where your money is.

Also, given the fact that FOREX is a 24-hour market, you can trade at any time. Most folks look into trading as a means of bringing in more money. Sure, it would be great to hit the jackpot and become a millionaire, but at least early on, that's not very likely. As such, looking to invest in FOREX early on as a part-time deal is a great way to find your footing.

There are plenty of folks who start in FOREX looking to earn an extra $200 or $300 a month. From there, you can increase your expectations, and perhaps bringing a couple of extra thousand dollars a month. If you put in the time and effort to become good at it, you can even make more than your regular salary. This is what enables some folks to become full-time traders. And while they may not become uber-wealthy, they make enough to earn a decent living.

CHAPTER 8:

Day Trading Options

When trading straight calls and puts, one of the best ways to earn profits is through day trading. Although options are not stocks, the same day trading rules apply to trading options as they do with stocks. It means that you have to know the definitions of a day trade and the legal requirements and risks.

Day trading options can be both desirable and lucrative because small price movements in stock, which happen all the time, are magnified in options. You can use day trading to get into options when prices are relatively low. Then you can get out when they reach a pricing level that represents an acceptable profit level for you on the same day before prices begin moving in the other direction again.

A $1 move in a stock price can represent a $10 to $100 move in an options price is what makes this approach very attractive. However, understanding how options are treated is important, as well. If you cannot meet the requirements for day trade options, you can still do it a few times a week, as we will discuss in a moment.

Options Tickers

Remember that each option has its ticker. This is important because day trading involves day traders of the same financial security. Once you buy and sell Apple stock on the same trading day, that is a day trade. However, buying and selling two different options on Apple stock does not constitute a day trade when it comes to options. To understand why, note that an option is defined on the underlying stock, in addition to the predetermined factors (strike and expiration). It also depends on the type of option. To continue our example above, a call option set at $240, with a deadline of 12/12/2019, is not the same financial security as a call option set at $240, with a deadline of 12/30/2019.

In the same breath, a call option with a strike price of $240 and an expiration date of 12/12/19 is not the same financial security as a put option expiring on 12/12/2019 with a predetermined $240 strike price.

So, the first thing to keep straight in your mind if you want to day trade options is the same financial security for day trading and what is not.

Day Trading: Defined

A day trade involves buying a stock or option and then selling that same stock or option before the close of the same trading day. Anyone is allowed to do a limited number of day trades, but what brokers and regulators are looking for is known as a pattern day trader. A pattern day trader, by definition, is someone that makes 4 or more day trades in any five days.

A five-day period means five consecutive trading days, so a weekend does not reset the counter. These days, most brokers will track the number of day trades you have in your account for you. So, when you are looking to make some trades but don't want to be labeled as a pattern day trader, you can make up to three-day trades, and then wait for the counter to drop to 2 or below.

Day Trader Requirements

Federal regulators consider day trading to be a high-risk activity. So, while it is legal, there are rules in place designed to keep day traders from causing brokers too much financial trouble should their trades go badly. The main rule you have to be aware of is that a day trader must have $25,000 deposited in their account. You also have to open a margin account. This is a large sum of money to put up for many people so that they might be effectively cut off from day trading. But if you can open a margin account and deposit the required sum, then you are free to enter into as many day trades as you like.

Of course, we hope that you won't be running out of the $25,000 if you choose this path, but becoming a day trader on an official basis will open up a lot more opportunities for you. Stocks are constantly moving up or down by small amounts, with trends that last a few hours or throughout the day that will generate large changes in options prices.

Getting rid of the day trade limitation not only lets you frequently trade, which will let you take advantage of more of these trends when you can spot them, but it will also allow you to make high-volume trades. Suppose you are subject to the day trading limitation, meaning you do not have a margin account with $25,000 in value in the account. In that case, you may get notices about day trading limitations if you try to trade multiple options in a single trade.

In other words, if you try trading 10 Apple options, all with the same strike price and expiration date, you might be told that you will not be allowed to sell all ten options on the same trading day. If you become an official day trader, then these restrictions would be lifted, giving you a lot more flexibility when trading.

Day Trading Without Becoming a Day Trader

If you cannot deposit $25,000 in a margin account or want to avoid becoming a pattern day trader, you can still use day trading as a part of a larger options trading strategy. In this case, you might want to trade options in a way that utilizes three or fewer-day trades in every five-trading day period. This can allow you to make three lucrative day trades per week to boost your overall trading revenues. The only issue with this type of trading activity is that you must avoid making too many day trades over a given five-business day period. If you are careful about avoiding this problem, this will not be an issue for you.

You can also effectively day trade by letting your trades run overnight. Technically speaking, this makes you a so-called "swing trader." A swing trader holds their positions overnight, for a few days, or even weeks. In practice, any options trader is a swing trader because all options contracts expire. So, in reality, there isn't any other way to be when trading options, except a day or swing trader.

If you are looking to day trade but want to avoid adding to your day trade account, there are two ways to go about doing it. The first way is to start in the morning looking for trends to trade on. Then you enter your trade and hold it overnight, provided that the profit you are going to make will account for the losses that could occur from theta or time decay.

So, if you've made $100 during the day, and theta is -0.12, you know that your profit is going to be automatically reduced by $12, but you might be willing to accept that small decline in profits. You can wait for the markets to close, and then enter an after-hours sale order, which will be executed at the market open. Or you can wait until the market opens before actually placing your order.

Alternatively, you can enter your positions just before the market close if you suspect a trend will carry through the following day. You will do this knowing that you will take a hit on the price of the option at the market open due to the theta or time decay.

This procedure can be very tricking, of course. The reason is that a lot of action can happen at the market open, and this can wipe out your positions if it is not something that works in your favor. For this reason, day traders of stocks don't hold positions overnight. But the risk with some options contracts will be lower than it would be trading a highly volatile penny stock the way that day traders of stocks do.

Remember the activity that takes place at the market open. Sometimes, even if you have placed an after-hours sale order, you might not be able to sell your option because prices are moving so fast at the market open. This may or may not happen, but you have to be aware of the possibility. That means that this is not a set-it-and-forget-it is a trading strategy. You will have to be on top of things, and actively following your trades at the market open if you need to cancel and replace an order.

Day Trading Options: The General Strategy

Now, let's consider this from the perspective of a trader who is going to straight-up day trade options. In this case, you will start in the morning and look for stocks that are entering a trend. Since you are trading options, which direction the trend is going is completely irrelevant. If the trend is down, buying put options is a legitimate way to earn profits.

You are going to want to look for signals that a new trend is forming. Sometimes, this can be after a trend reversal. A trend reversal can occur after a large selloff of stocks occurs, and the stock enters oversold conditions. This is a time to buy shares as the stock will probably reverse and start increasing in price. Or, in the case of trading options, you are going to want to buy call options.

Of course, the trend that is forming may be a reversal of an uptrend. So, the stock may be overbought, and there might have been a long upward trend in price, but now, it's showing signals of declining. In that case, you are going to want to buy put options.

A large trend reversal isn't necessary either. Look for signs in the stock charts that an upward trend is forming. This can be high risk, and it's awfully hard to predict when a trend is forming accurately, but with practice, many traders can get quite good at it. When the signals are there, you can then buy options that fit the trend you are looking for.

CHAPTER 9:

Binary Options Trading

A Binary Option is a method for investing in an asset price that has just two closing positions. A wise investment can be made if the closing area is estimated precisely.

The most widely recognized option is the "High" or "Low" option. To begin, an understanding of the time length is fixed before making the expectation. The trader can anticipate a fixed return if, toward the end, the price lies on the right side of the started price.

The trader will lose the entirety he invested when the trade was opened if predicted incorrectly.

With an itemized investigation into buying and selling stocks, the straightforwardness at which one can place trades using Binary Options ends up visible.

An investor starts trading by selecting and purchasing a measure of a stock or an asset. By calculating the offer price individually, we can ascertain what the price of the asset is.

A trader can produce a decent return by selling his asset when the price has risen from the asset's price at the outset. In like manner, the investor will encounter a loss if the asset's selling price is not the exact price it was acquired.

Complete learning and experience of numerous outcomes are fundamental to invest in these lines — an intensive understanding of how the financial market capacity is critical. The investor would need to examine the asset's price movements, how price-changing occasions influence the asset in the market, and how the asset's price will change in the future.

To effectively bring these components together, the investor who routinely creates gainful returns identifies and understands asset price switches, and is sponsored by trading strategies and methods that can be actualized when the circumstance requests it.

Having no technique or understanding of assets, and the market may leave you in your very own private sorrow what you have saved for investing will before long vanish. You won't have adequate assets to buy presents for the children at Christmas, and your accomplice may keep running off with somebody more proficient at investing their money than yourself!

What is appealing in the examination is that there is no compelling reason to buy into anything when investing with Binary Options. Binary investments highlight prices of assets, and if the price of an asset will rise or fall. For this situation, you are trading exclusively on an up or down movement in an asset's price. Consequently, it is an impressively less unsafe investment opportunity.

Likewise, it is deserving of note that Binary Options Trading enables potential investors to get up, and running without putting down enormous entireties to begin because the required investment sum can be a lot smaller.

If an investor were looking to start trading on gold, which depended on the present estimation of gold, it would make it exceptionally difficult for many people to make it an advantageous asset to invest in. In Binary Options Trading, nobody is genuinely buying any gold; instead, traders invest in price changes of gold over a set time frame.

Assets Available to Trade with Binary Options

Before we talked about gold, now would be a good time to dig into the sorts of assets regularly utilized for Binary Options Trading.

- Indices: An index is simply the market. It is conceivable to invest in the markets themselves.

- Forex: Or Foreign Exchange is worried about trade rates between significant currency sets, for example, the USD, the GBP, or the JP. You can trade on combinations of all these real monetary forms.

- Commodities: A crude material or essential rural item that can be purchased or sold, for example, Gold, Copper, or Coffee.

Selecting which asset to trade is the starting point for a trader. The magnificence of Binary Options Trading is as natural as getting up and run.

Getting Started

Most trading stages give two necessary decisions regarding binary trading: The put option is chosen if the trader accepts that the cost will decline, while the call option is accessible. If they receive that, the price will rise. All traders need to choose their position depending on any number of market factors. There are various trading methods and calculations that can be utilized, which will be secured later.

Before choosing your position, you will be required to pick a trading stage to direct most of your trades. Selecting the correct broker to deal with your finances is essential to accomplishing your trades, particularly for new traders who need to benefit as much as possible from every single financial option. Not all brokers will most likely give you similar trading methods, much like not all brokers will have similar restrictions and profits accessible for their sites. New traders are prescribed not to stress over a portion of the more confounded binary trading methods. First, pick a decent brokerage that offers a high rate on their profits, and check whether there are any incentive projects offered that you can exploit.

Tips to Keep in Mind

There is a wide range of tips and deceives that beginning traders can remember to increase their odds of profiting. A considerable amount of these tips is additionally intended to enable individuals to be more open to the trading background, particularly if they need a couple of dependable guidelines to remember as they trade. As the trader becomes increasingly experienced, they will most likely build up their trading methods and frames of mind, which are explicitly structured to supplement their very own remarkable way of dealing with trading. Until further notice, in any case, merely remembering a couple of these essential tips can be enough to enable most traders to get a head start.

Let Emotions well enough alone for Your Trades

Maybe the most crucial suggestion to recollect is to never depend on hunches or natural desires. Trading binary options don't care for gambling or some other essential money-making process. While chance still assumes a job in determining your profits, most of them will be identified via deliberately examined indicators and adequately actualized strategies. Traders who depend on their instincts or any passionate associations with their finances will find that they will begin losing money in the long term, regardless of what inadvertent profits they may verify from the start.

Making genuinely determined trades is an extremely massive slip-up that, shockingly, numerous section level traders make. If your head isn't clear and you are not thinking objectively, you will wind up making trading botches. It is as straightforward as that. If you begin to feel baffled or irate with your trades or become too energized after successful ones, it is essential to take a step back, take a full breath, and think about taking a break.

Think About Yourself as a Trader

The best traders are simply the ones who know and realize what they need to escape their trades. These individuals have investigated different types of options, and have chosen to work with ones that match their characters as traders. Short-term trades are identified by brisk exchanges in unstable situations, such as sixty second and two-minute trades. Medium-term trades allude to any exchanges that can be made somewhere in the range of five and fifteen minutes. As the name infers, long-term trades depict more extended expiry periods, which can go anyplace from an hour to multi-day, depending on the broker.

As should be evident from the range, there is a way to deal with each type, which defines the trader. If you flourish in quick paced situations and enjoy the dangers of dealing with instability, you will be more qualified to work with short term trades. Then again, if you enjoy a lower level of risk, and plan on trading consistently if possible, you may profit from more extended expiry options.

CHAPTER 10:

How to Get Maximum Profits

You Can Profit from Any Market Situation

It is to benefit from any market situation trading options. Most options strategies are carried out by combining different option positions, and sometimes even the underlying stock's position. A trading strategy can be used singly or in combination with others to profit from market situations.

You stand to make huge profits with options trading, yet your risk and exposure are limited. Ordinary stock trading does not afford you such opportunities. The most crucial aspects of options trading know when to exit a trade, and how to exit. Knowing how and when to exit is vital for successful trading.

Options strategies are the most versatile strategies in the financial markets. They provide traders and investors with numerous profit-making opportunities with limited exposure and risk. These strategies can be favorable whether the underlying security's stock price rises, remains the same, or falls.

Taking Profits with Options Trading

One of the best-known ways of profiting from options is through the purchase of undervalued options. You can even buy options at the right price and still benefit from them.

Options prices usually are extremely volatile. This provides an excellent chance to benefit from profit-taking. However, when you miss the right moment to take profits, you will have lost out on an amazing opportunity.

Take Advantage of Volatility and Collect Profits

Options are unlike stocks because they have a time limit. Stocks can be held indefinitely, but options can expire. This means that the time for trades is limited. As a trader, you cannot afford to miss this window. Should such a chance be missed, then it might not be seen again in a long while.

You should avoid long-term strategies when trading options. Strategies such as the average are unsuitable for options trading because of the limited time that options have. Also, watch out for margin requirements. Such requirements have to capacity to severely impact your trading funds requirements.

Watch out for multiple factors that may affect a favorable price. For instance, the price of the underlying stock may go up, which is a good thing. However, other factors, such as dividend payment, time decay, or volatility, may erode any accruing benefit. Such constraints make it imperative that you learn to follow profit-taking strategies. Here are some of these crucial profit-taking strategies that you can use as a trader.

Trailing Stop Strategy

When using this strategy, you will set a pre-determined percentage for a particular target. For instance, you can ten options contracts, each costing $80 with a profit target of $100 and a $70 stop-loss.

Set a Profit-Taking Stop-Loss

We can set a stop-loss at 5%, which means if our target price of $100 is attained, our trailing target will be $95. If the upward trend continues and our price gets to $120, then the trailing target of 5% becomes $114. Should the price movement continue to, say, $150, then the trailing target this time becomes $142.5.

Should the price now start falling, you will exit and collect profits at this $142.5. The trailing stop lets you enjoy protection as the price increases, and then exits a trade once the price turns around. The stop-loss levels should neither be too small nor too large. If they are too small, they will cause frequent triggers, whereas too large will make profit-taking unachievable.

Partial Profit Booking

Season traders have a routine that they follow to book partial profits. First, they set a target and take profits when it is attained.

Partial profit booking helps to protect the trader's capital to a large extent. This essentially has the effect of preventing capital losses in the event of a sudden price change. Such price reversals are commonly observed in options trading.

Book Partial Profits at Regular Time Intervals

As a trader, you can book partial profits at regular time intervals. However, you will need to pay close attention to the time limit. A massive portion of your options premium is made of its time value. As time runs out, then its value also goes down. As a trader, you should keep a keen eye on your options' time value as this erodes its value. Buyers should be careful about the time limit.

Sell Covered Call Options against Long Positions

Selling options is a lucrative income-generating process. This is not the only pathway to riches in the markets. You can also sell naked puts. This is like selling shares or stocks that you do not.

When you sell naked put options, you will free up your time to do a lot more. Stock trading allows you to sell stocks of shares that you do not have for a profit. This tends to free up your capital so you can invest it or trade with it indefinitely. It is advisable to stick to stocks that you understand very well, and those you would not mind. There is still hedging associated with options trading, so always be careful and watch about that. Most large investors who deal in options are often hedging.

Consider all the Options Available to You

We make assumptions that traders will hold their positions until the end. You can choose from several options to ensure that you can leverage any time you want to see its need.

Learn to Select the Right Options to Trade

You have to identify options that will see you earn a profit.

- Ensure you determine whether you are bullish or bearish on the market, sector, or just the stock. When you make these decisions, you will be able to identify the options you wish to buy.

- Consider volatility and think about how it would affect your options trading strategy. Think about the status of the market. Is it calm, or is it volatile? You may also want to consider the expiration date and strike price. If you only have a couple of shares, this would be a great time and opportunity to purchase more stock.

CHAPTER 11:

Stock Market

The stock market is the place you can purchase and trade stocks on any business day. It's also called a stock trade.

Why Companies Sell Stocks

Organizations sell stocks to get brokers to grow bigger. When individuals need to begin a business, they frequently pay for it with individual loans or even their credit cards. When they develop the organization enough, they can get bank loans. They can also sell bonds to individual investors.

In the end, they'll need a great deal of cash to take the business to the following stage. Around then, they will sell the main stocks, called an initial public offering. When that occurs, no single individual owns the organization since they have sold it to the stockholders. Since the U.S. stock market is so modern, it is simpler in this nation than in many others to take a company public. It enables the economy to extend since it gives a lift up to companies wishing to grow huge.

The requirement for organizations to raise money and investors to profit from them keeps the stock market up.

Why Invest in the Stock Market?

Stock market investing is the ideal approach to accomplish returns that beat inflation over time. There are four different advantages to investing.

1. Stock ownership exploits a developing economy.
2. Unlike brokers, it's anything but difficult to purchase stocks and just as simple to sell.
3. The best part is that you can make money in two different ways. A few investors like to let their stock appreciate over time.
4. Others favor stocks that deliver dividends to give a consistent income stream.

There different ways for you to invest in the stock market. The quickest and least expensive is to buy them online. If you need more direction at a sensible value, join an investment club. A full-service broker will cost all the more, however, would value the price. The person will give you proficient suggestions. A money manager charges the most yet will accomplish all the work for you.

Rather than purchasing singular stocks, you could get them as part of an index fund or a mutual fund. An index fund follows a guide, for example, the MSCI developing market index. A mutual fund has a manager that purchases the stocks for you. The most dangerous is the hedge fund. They invest likewise in derivatives, which could build the return and increase the risk.

Investing Risks

The most note value downside is that you can lose your whole investment if the stock value falls to zero. If the organization goes bankrupt, stock investors are paid after bondholders. Thus, stock investing can be an emotional rollercoaster. If you need guaranteed returns, stick to bonds. Be that as it may, stocks are a superior approach if you are in it as long as possible.

When stock market costs decay under 10% that is known as a stock market revision. When costs fall that much or more in one day, it's known as a stock market crash. When costs fall 20% or more, it's known as a bear advertise. These usually last 18 months. The inverse is a bull market, and they last two to five years.

The U.S. Stock market is the World's Financial Capital

The United States is in the area of the two biggest trades on the planet. The New York Stock Trade accounts for 2,400 organizations. The estimated value is at around $21 trillion in market capitalization. The NYSE is arranged on Wall Street. The NASDAQ companies with a market top of $11 trillion. It's arranged in Times Square. Both are in Manhattan, New York.

The stock market works by coordinating buyers and dealers. The two significant trades do it any other way from one another. The NYSE is a genuine auction house. It coordinates the most note Value offer at the least sales price. A market producer for each stock will fill in the hole to guarantee exchanges go without any problem. At the NASDAQ, purchasers and merchants exchange with a seller as opposed to each other. It's done electronically, so exchanges happen in split seconds.

The United States is the world's monetary capital since its financial markets are so advanced. Therefore, as a result, information on companies is easy to obtain. This transparency builds the trust of investors from around the globe. Thus, the U.S. stock market draws in more investors. That makes it much simpler for a U.S. organization to open up to the world.

The general U.S. stock market presentation is followed by its three head accounts: the Dow Jones Industrial Average, the S&P 500, and the NASDAQ. Various parts of the markets are also followed. For instance, the MSCI Index tracks stocks' presentation in developing market countries, for example, China, India, and Brazil.

Major World Stock Markets

Each significant nation has a stock trade. Here are the best 10, positioned by total market capitalization. They are accounted with the most quoted indices that are nearest to estimating their performances:

- New York Stock Trade – NYSE.

- NASDAQ - The trade likewise has an account with a similar name.

- Tokyo Stock Trade - Nikkei 225.

- London Stock Trade - FTSE 100.

- Shanghai Stock Trade - Shanghai Stock Trade.

- Hong Kong Stock Trade - Hang Seng.

- Toronto Stock Trade - SPTSX.

- Bombay Stock Trade - SENSEX.

- National Stock Trade of India - NSE Nifty.

- BM&F Bo Vespa (Brazil) - The file is additionally called BOVESPA.

Other Financial Markets

The stock market is only one type of financial market. Before you invest, ensure you know about them all:

Items are generally traded in future options, which makes them increasingly confounded. They incorporate grains, oil, and the abnormally named pork bellies.

Foreign trade is the place individuals purchase and sell currencies. It's high risk because the qualities can change drastically for no evident explanation and change rapidly.

Derivatives are exceptionally complicated bonds that get their incentive from the hidden resources, for example, subprime mortgages. Singular investors should remain away. Although they can give huge returns and can also reduce your entire life savings in a day.

Supply and Demand

If an organization reports shockingly low profit, demand for its stock may fade, and as the value drops, the harmony among buyers and sellers is changed. Buyers will begin mentioning discount on the present cost, and many prodded sellers will oblige them to dispose of the stocks. Once there are more sellers than buyers, this generates more supply than demand, so the value starts to fall.

The Role of Prices

Eventually, a stock's cost may drop to a level where buyers find it attractive, or some other factor will change the dynamic. As buyers move into the market, demand becomes quicker than supply, and the expense correspondingly goes up. Sometimes supply and demand discover a balance, a value that purchasers acknowledge, and that seller obliges. Costs will bounce up and down when market supply and demand are generally equivalent, yet they will do it in a narrow price range. It's workable for stock to remain in this range for a considerable length of time or even a very long time before another outside factor disturbs the supply and demand balance, and causes either a perceptible increase or decrease in cost.

If interest for a stock surpasses the supply, its cost will rise, yet it will just increment to a point where buyers speculate that demand is disappearing. By then, holders of the stock will probably start selling. Some may have ridden the cost up and accept an inversion is coming, so they sell their shares and take their benefits while they are still ahead.

When stock costs start to fall (which can occur for a few reasons), and more owners begin selling their shares, there will be more supply than there is demand. To tempt buyers, sellers must drop costs to oblige the saturated market. A similar unique deal with the opposite side, however, is a switch. As the value falls, it will arrive at a level that buyers find attractive. As buyers get shares, the stock's cost will rise because sellers must be lured to let go of their shares.

Understanding Stock Market Fluctuations

It is surely known that the stock market is unstable and hard to anticipate. What is less well understood is why. What are the raw sources of economic factors that drive these sporadic changes? By a long shot, most of the discourse in the press, additionally most economic hypotheses, declares that the market is driven by shocks (erratic variances) to macroeconomic basics that have significant consequences for economic growth. The most significant irregular powers behind the more drawn out term gains in the U.S. stock exchange have not been drivers of financial development. However, it has rather been an aggregation of irregular shocks to a great extent uncorrelated with economic development that has brought about redistribution among laborers and investors.

There is a little puzzle that the genuine estimation of the stock market floats upward over significant stretches to a great extent unsurprising path as efficiency (driven by innovative advancement) improves. Likewise, this same deterministic pattern has pushed yield per capita, and the average way of life upward in the course of the last several centuries. It is rather the random shocks, the bloom, and busts around this trend, about which we have little information, yet on which a continuous stream of media theory centers. Such random shocks can steadily displace the market from its long-term pattern for periods up to quite a few years.

CHAPTER 12:

The Benefit of Having a Good Mental Attitude as a Trader

If you have decided to get into trading, then it only means one thing. Your mind lives to analyze, and you are fascinated by monetary trends. This alone gives every beginner an edge over those who do not. You do not need to worry if you are a beginner. At least you are doing what most are not.

The mind of every trader needs not only to be fast but also laser-focused. This is because, in the instance of day trading, the whole dance happens in one song. Meaning, all the money you invest in has the chance to multiply or decrease all in one day.

Resilience is an excellent mental attitude that all traders must abide by. Some days you make incredible profits, and the stocks are all in your favor. Other days, not so much, and you end up feeling worse when you exit than when entering. The art of resilience, to say to yourself that you will try again tomorrow, is essential.

Discipline with your account is also another vital attitude a trader should have. This is helpful while buying stocks as they experience a losing streak, and then one might be tempted to use more than they had planned. Learn to discipline the mind in stopping to avoid heavy losses.

Every trader must be high on caution. Eagerness tends to be the greatest mistake that ruins not only traders but also big companies. This is because in the race to make more money, one tends to overlook a few things that might cause him more harm than good in the stock market. Pausing and observing is important as it helps avoid risky money behavior.

Helps You Achieve Your Goals

Your thoughts are essential in shaping your life and ensuring that you accomplish the goals that you have set. As humans, we like making specific goals for our lives, and you might have set that at a certain time, and you want to earn a certain amount of money. As a day trader, you might be having some goals on the amount of money you wish to correct at the end of the day. These goals are good as they keep you motivated.

Ensure that You Stay Focused

A positive mental attitude can have a huge impact on your ability to focus. Set your mind to achieving something, then constantly remind yourself to give your best to achieve what you have planned to get. This can be done by having some daily affirmations. You will be surprised by the impact that these affirmations will have on your life. Every day that you wake up say something good about yourself. Remind yourself that you can tune your mind into focusing on the plans you have for the day.

Increases Your Potential of Earning an Income

It is amazing how our thoughts influence our level of productivity. When we have a positive attitude, our productivity levels are likely to increase. The vice versa is also applicable. When our thoughts are negative, we are likely to experience a decrease in our level of production. As a trader, you need a positive mental attitude as you conduct your trades.

It Minimizes Stress Levels

At times life can move quickly, and you are not adequately prepared for it. You may feel overwhelmed as it could result in stress. When it gets to some extreme levels, the stress can result in something major like trauma. We have had people engage in day trading to encounter a loss at the end of a trade. You will find that some invested in more than they could afford. Some traders borrow loans so that they can trade.

Helps You Know How to Handle Failure

As a trader, not every day will be a celebration day. Some days you will win, and on other days you will lose. You cannot get in a trade with a full guarantee that things will go as you planned. You will often come across some losses, and there is no need to feel overwhelmed by the losses. With the help of a positive mental attitude, you can avoid some of these frustrations. All you have to do is tune your mind to having the right positive attitude. It makes you ready in case anything happens.

Provides Room for Growth

One of the beautiful things about life is that it allows us to grow. One can experience growth in all aspects of their life. For you to grow, you require a positive mental attitude. It propels you towards success in life and allows you to make the right choices and decisions. As a beginner in day trading, you will have to learn a lot of things. Some of these things you will have to teach yourself. Your performance will be influenced by how much you know, and how willing you are to learn.

Helps You in Taking Care of Your Emotions

Emotions are part of who we are. Someone might tell you something that upsets you, and your emotion is ruined. At that point, you can become sad or angered. If you achieve something good, you automatically become happy and proud of yourself. On a good day, you may have made several trades and acquired a huge profit. This is something that you will feel happy and proud of. It can automatically bring you in a cheerful mood, and you will feel so good about your success.

Allows You to Be Hopeful

As a beginner, you will come across numerous challenges while trading options. It is entirely up to you to ensure that these challenges do not interfere with your growth and general output. You need to reenergize constantly so that the challenges become bearable. One of the benefits of having a positive mental attitude is that it allows one to be hopeful. You believe that things will get better with each passing day. This will boost your confidence, and enable you to get better at what you do. This attitude will be helpful while trading options.

Helps You in Making Sound Decisions

While day trading, there are a lot of decisions that you will make. Some of these decisions will determine if you expose yourself to more risks or make a profit or a loss. A single decision can make your investment worth your while or make you lose all you have worked hard for. While trading, there are several factors that you will have to consider. These factors determine if you will make a profit or make a loss. When it comes to selecting the appropriate option strategy, one needs to make a lot of choices.

You Learn from Your Failures

No one gets in anything with the expectations of failing. You find that you have an exam, and even though you have not adequately prepared for it, you still expect to pass. As entrepreneurs establish various businesses, their end goal is to become successful at what they do and get profits at the end of the day. We have people engaging in options trading to generate an income. No one enters a trade with the expectation that they will fail.

CHAPTER 13:

What Every Investor Should Do

While all the information in this guide should prepare you to enter the world of options trading with some degree of confidence, nothing can prepare you for live trading. Every situation will be different and may require any one of the strategies or some combination of them. However, no one can prepare any options trader for every conceivable transaction, event, or opportunity. Success in this field will come with the continued application of the methods, strategies, and knowledge you have learned.

This includes what we consider to be the most important do's and don'ts of options trading. We hope not only that you put these strategies to work, but also that you start formulating your compilation of road-tested options trading secrets.

Understand Market Basics

In the modern world, investment has been made accessible to the average person. Most employers who offer retirement savings plans often sponsor an education day, so employees can gain some familiarity with the types of retirement plans and available options. Also, with the proliferation of cable news networks, specialized programming, the internet, and social media, there is no shortage of information widely available to virtually anyone, anywhere.

Especially in the information age, knowledge is power. Before you jump right into trading on the options market, take some time to familiarize yourself with market dynamics basics. Options traders use a unique language to their niche in the investment world, and many outsiders may be completely perplexed and unable to understand much of what they say. The ability to tolerate a certain amount of financial risk is an inseparable component of successful investing. Thus, by understanding the terminology of the options market and the fundamental dynamics of the stock market in general, investors can exponentially increase their chances of assembling a profitable career in options trading.

Play by the Rules

As an options trader, you will compete with other traders and investors. Much of your success in investing, including making valuable connections in the investment world, will result from your ability to play by the rules. The stock market is a living thing, and traders' activity has a significant impact on its health and volatility. We are all tempted to be maverick investors who leave a legacy of innovation but understanding the fundamentals will work in your favor.

Specifically, option prices increase or decrease as a result of changes in share prices and volatility.

When share prices increase, call options to make money and put options to lose money; when share prices decrease, put options make money and call options to lose money. Options also move to volatility; when share prices are stable, greater volatility can increase option pricing. So, when volatility rises, buying options make money; when volatility decreases, selling options makes money.

Understanding these four basic rules can help you become a better trader.

Adapt Your Strategy to Market Conditions

Once you're up and running in the world of professional options trading, you will gain confidence as you see your efforts pay off in returns to your options account. As you move from a Level 1 trading account to a Level 2 trading account, you will likely develop a preference for a certain type of options trades, maybe covered calls or married puts. Familiarity with the language and mechanics of the options trading profession is something that will work in your favor. However, it is important to remember that you will gain access to a wider array of trading tools and strategies as you move up the ladder.

As you gain knowledge and experience, remember that no matter how comfortable you have become with a select number of options trading strategies, there will always be additional aspects of nuance that can enhance your skill as a trader and increase your efforts' profitability. The key to ensuring success is not just choosing the best strategy for the underlying asset's performance.

You must also consider the overall market conditions, and whether those conditions may affect that asset's future performance. Although one strategy may have worked in the past under similar conditions, considering changes in current conditions will help you adjust your strategy to ensure you continue to build on your past success.

Always Have an Exit Plan

Picking a stock, formulating an options strategy to generate income from the stock's performance, and then contacting your broker to initiate an opening transaction is a good beginning. But this plan is not a complete strategy. The most important part of any options strategy is not how to get in; it's how to get out.

The payoff of an options strategy may result from buying the underlying stock at below market value, from accepting a cash settlement deposit for a put option on the stock with declining value, or even from profiting from an increase in the cost of the options premium by selling the contract before it expires. However, you believe the asset you have identified may provide you with an opportunity to construct a profitable options trading strategy, conjecture, and hope should not be part of that strategy.

Before you complete an opening transaction, make sure you know your specific goal for entering the contract. After you complete the opening transaction, you will be faced with one of three possible outcomes:

- The market and the target stocks moved in the direction you predicted.

- The market or the target stocks move in a direction you did not predict, resulting in unexpected losses.

- The market or the target stocks move in a direction you did not predict, resulting in unexpected gains.

Conclusion

I hope this guide will teach you everything you need to know about options trading, from basics, why people trade options, and how you trade options. It will teach you everything you need to know on this important topic so that you can start making money right now with options trading without having any knowledge at all. You will find out precisely what kinds of investments there are available, and exactly how much your broker will charge for each one so that you can choose the one that is best for your situation.

It is a great way to make money through leverage. With options, you can make money by selling an asset at a specific price and buying it back after rising in price. It's an exciting and profitable way to gain financial freedom. The options market is the largest and most liquid market globally, which means that it is also very popular. Options trading is an attractive option for anyone looking to make money from their investments. It's a way of investing in stocks or other securities without actually having to buy them.

Options' trading allows you to make money and increase your wealth. There are many different types of options, but most people are familiar with the call option. It is one of the best ways to make money in the stock market. Options are contracts that give you the right, but not the obligation, to buy or sell an asset at a specified price within a specific time frame. Options trading is one of the most popular ways for traders to earn money.

Options trading is a great way to make money while watching the markets. Although options trading can be a complicated process, there are plenty of resources to help you get started.

This can be a great way to make money, but it's essential to do your research and know what you're doing. It is one of the most fun and lucrative forms of investing, but it's also one of the most challenging. The goal of options trading is to buy stock or other assets at a price you think will go up in the future.

The Options Trading Crash Course is a great place to start. The course walks you through the basics of options trading and teaches all the concepts you need to know.